BLADING

Martin Smith

W
HODDER
Wayland

An imprint of Hodder Children's Books

to the limit

BLADING

Other titles in this well-cool series are:

MOTOCROSS

MOUNTAIN BIKING

SKATEBOARDING

SNOWBOARDING

SURFING

Prepared for Hodder Wayland by Roger Coote Publishing, Gissings Farm, Fressingfield, Suffolk IP21 5SH

© Hodder Wayland 2000

Project Management: Mason Editorial Services
Designer: Tim Mayer

Published in 2000 by
Hodder Wayland, an imprint of
Hodder Children's Books

A Catalogue record for this book is available from the British Library.

ISBN 0 7502 2782 6
Printed and bound by G. Canale & CSpA, Turin, Italy

Hodder Children's Books
A division of Hodder Headline Limited
338 Euston Road, London NW1 3BH

WARNING!
Blading is a dangerous sport. This book is full of advice, but reading it won't keep you safe. Take responsibility for your own safety.

WHAT IS BLADING?

When you first get a pair of blades, the front door of your home becomes a doorway to another world. You will never see your surroundings in the same way again. Your first wobble on a pair of blades starts you on a quest to find the smoothest routes through the streets. Soon you're sweeping downhill or pulling radical airs.

Most people start blading with a gentle cruise around the park on a borrowed or rented pair of blades. But once you've mastered the basic blading skills, you'll find your pulse rate and your speed levels rising.

Blading tech talk

Hard boot – Similar in design to a ski boot, gives lots of support (good for beginners).

Soft boot – Boot made from soft trainer-type materials, advantages are: breathable, light and good to look at.

Chassis – The under-boot frame in which the wheels are held.

Bearings – Tiny metal balls inside the wheels which help them to roll faster.

ABEC rating – Manufacturers give bearings a number to indicate how accurately they are made (higher number means more accurate, faster bearing).

Foot bed – Soft foam sheet that can be placed under the foot; installing a better one is the easiest way to improve any skate.

Bladers enjoying the sunshine.

The four kinds of blading:

- **Recreational:** blading for fitness and fun.
- **Aggressive/street:** performing tricks and jumps on obstacles in skate parks or the street.
- **Hockey:** like ice hockey but on blades.
- **Speed:** blading as fast as you can downhill.

History

The idea of taking the grace of skating outside the ice rink is not a recent one. Designs for blades have been around since the 1820s, but it wasn't until the early 1980s that the first modern versions were produced.

Turning theory

Basic blading turns are called edged turns. Each blade has an inside edge (the same side as the big toe), and an outside edge (the little toe). It is the use of edges that links blading to skiing and ice skating. Watch bladers doing a series of slalom turns: they have the same body positions as a downhill skier.

Wall rides like this one require speed and confidence.

Below: Tricks like this one are a fairly recent invention.

Above: Bladers building their own mini-ramp.

Scott and Brennan Olson, two ice hockey players from Minneapolis, U.S.A., used hockey-type boots, a rigid chassis and urethane wheels to make the first-ever blades. Before long, people all over the U.S.A. realised that wide, smooth walkways, particularly those of the coastal towns, were ideal places to blade. Skiers, ice skaters and hockey players appreciated the chance to do a similar sport outdoors in the summer sunshine. Other people caught on too, and soon blading spread to Europe and beyond.

Rough Riders

Early blades manufactured by people like Robert John Tyres were not hugely popular, probably because they had iron wheels!

Equipment

Each style of blading makes different demands on equipment. Recreational bladers want to be able to wear skates for hours on end. Hockey bladers want to turn sharply; aggressive and street bladers need grind area. Some skates allow you to cross from one style of blading to another. But it is important to get the right skate for the type of skating you do most often.

Recreational blades

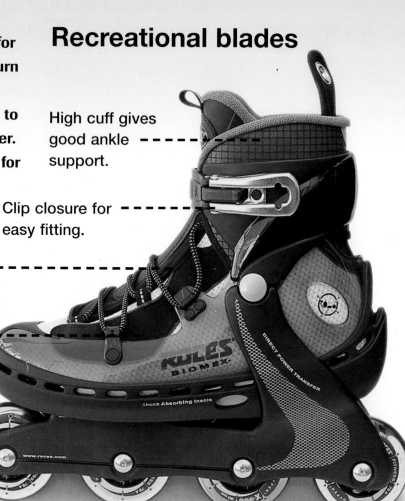

High cuff gives good ankle support.

Clip closure for easy fitting.

Inner boot thickly padded for comfort.

Perforated boots are cool and light.

Big wheels for higher speed.

Bearings

The bearings inside the wheels have a major effect on performance. Get the best bearings you can afford. High-quality bearings cost more but they last longer and are faster. Also, look after your bearings – remember, water and bearings do not mix. Take off your skates if it starts to rain.

Aggressive skate

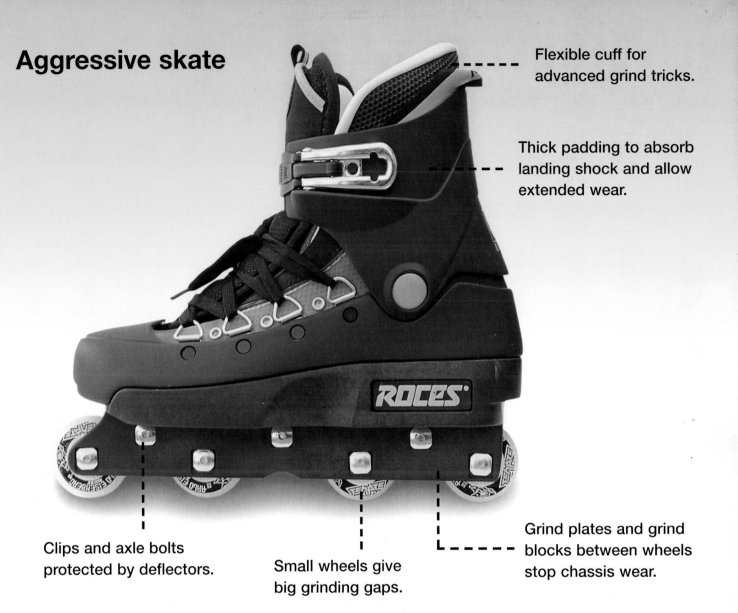

Flexible cuff for advanced grind tricks.

Thick padding to absorb landing shock and allow extended wear.

Clips and axle bolts protected by deflectors.

Small wheels give big grinding gaps.

Grind plates and grind blocks between wheels stop chassis wear.

Hockey skates:

Low cuff allows flexibility for turning; mid-sized, soft wheels for sharp turns and good grip; less padding gives more accurate edge control; lace closure allows tighter fitting.

Speed skates

Ultra-low cuff allows extended stride length; fifth wheel for extreme speed; lightweight, rigid chassis minimises power loss due to flex; lace closure allows tight fit.

9

Equipment 2

Safety equipment is important for bladers. The amount of padding you wear should always reflect the worst-case scenario for the type of skating that you are doing. Even the most experienced bladers take a fall once in a while. Remember, when things go wrong on skates, they go wrong very quickly.

Minimum requirements

Recreational blading

Wrist guards and knee pads (learners should add elbow pads and a helmet).

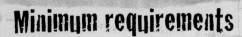

Standard helmet

Aggressive blading

Wrist guards; knee and elbow pads are much thicker than recreational pads, to spread the load of a fall from a great height; helmet. Perhaps shin guards and a 'nappy' (a pair of padded shorts).

Hockey

Wrist, knee and elbow pads are the minimum. Hockey clubs will insist that bladers wear full protection during a game – upper and lower body armour, padded gloves, a face visor and gum shield.

Speed skating

The need to keep an aerodynamic shape means that padding is kept to a minimum. Wrist guards and a helmet are an essential requirement, but with just these an accident can be very dangerous.

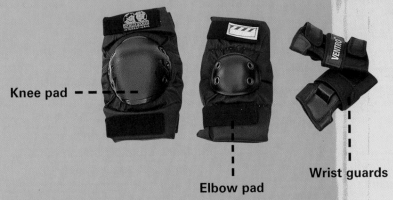

Knee pad

Elbow pad

Wrist guards

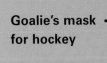

Goalie's mask for hockey

Wrist guards

Protection Guidelines

- No amount of protection is too much.
- Think about the skating that you will be doing, and imagine the type of accident that you may have.
- Get fully padded up before practising new moves.

BASIC techniques

Heel braking

1

Brake control is the hardest basic blading skill to learn. Your body's natural reaction when things start to go wrong is to tense up. This causes your knees to straighten and your head to pull back, which is the opposite of good braking technique. So, the first rule is to stay calm.

All beginner blades have a heel brake: this is a large rubber block at the back of one blade. There is more than one way to stop, but heel braking is the first method to learn because it's the easiest. More advanced ways of stopping, like the T-stop and the power slide, require advanced skills.

Slide the braking foot out in front of the supporting blade.

2

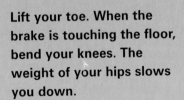

Lift your toe. When the brake is touching the floor, bend your knees. The weight of your hips slows you down.

3

Top tip

If you are worried about putting blades on for the very first time, make use of the anti-rolling properties of carpet. When wearing blades on carpet you'll be able to walk around and get a feel for the weight of the blades. When you feel confident, move outside.

Keep everything – knees, shoulders and head – forward. Stretching your arms straight out in front will bring even more weight forward.

Try to keep the braking foot out in front. If you let it slip back alongside your supporting foot, you will not stop.

The power slide braking technique needs a lot of balance and good edge control. Practise blading on one foot and backwards to obtain the skills needed.

AGGRESSIVE skating

You don't have to be aggressive to be an aggressive skater! But aggressive bladers do have a different attitude to their sport. To experienced aggressive bladers, the urban environment is an adventure park, full of wild rides. Stairs, rails, curbs and benches are not obstacles but opportunities for tricks and grinds.

The move that sets aggressive blading apart from all other styles is the grind. Grinds can be performed on curbs, benches, handrails – anything that will slide on a part of the skate. Remember, though: if it's hard enough to grind, it's hard enough to hurt. When learning aggressive skating it's especially important to wear a helmet, because the back of your head is very exposed if you fall backwards.

Anthony Mackie: Torque Soul (a kind of grind).

Grind terms

Frontside grind – With the rail on your right, turn 90 degrees to the right when you jump on to it.

Backside – Turn 90 degrees to the left.

50-50 – Both feet placed 90 degrees to the rail, grinding between the middle wheels.

Sole grind – Front foot across the rail, rear foot in line with the rail sliding on the outside sole of the boot.

Unity – Both skates in line with rail on outside soles.

Nollie – Grinding between first and second wheel.

Jenny Logue: Fishbrain (grind).

Mike Morales: Rocket Fishbrain (grind).

Richard Taylor: Wall ride.

Jon Julio: Fahrvergnügen (grind).

Getting Air

Jumping, or 'getting air', is a basic skill that all aggressive bladers need to master. To start with, you will get air when you jump on and off a grind rail, but leaving the ground is only the start of getting air. Spins, flips and grabs give extra style to tricks and in competitions big, stylish airs score more points.

How to air

1 Place the ramp somewhere with plenty of space. Start by rolling up to the ramp very slowly and turning on the ramp. Roll out facing back the way you came. This will familiarise you with the feel of the ramp.

2 Skate to the ramp with plenty of speed and 'pop' up as you reach the lip. 'Popping' means straightening your knees and is basically a small jump.

3 Once you are confident in the air you can start to experiment with different tricks.

4 Bend your knees and keep your weight forward for the landing. Roll out from the landing.

5 Look out for obstacles like lampposts: you may be travelling quite fast!

Big Air

The official world record for getting air on blades is 2.7 metres, by Raphael Sandoz of Switzerland.

Skate parks

The skate park is the safest place to learn aggressive skating, meet other people who are into the same kind of skating and see new manoeuvres.

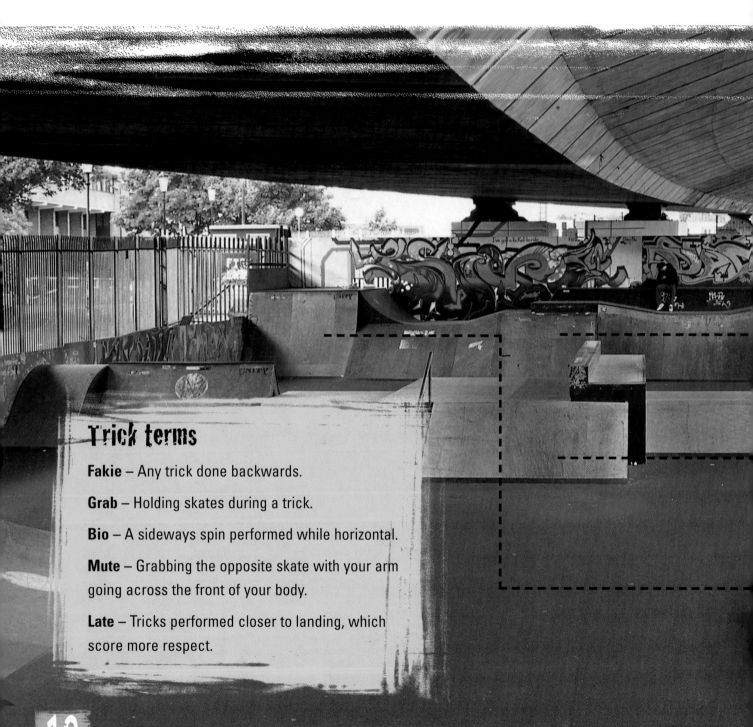

Trick terms

Fakie – Any trick done backwards.

Grab – Holding skates during a trick.

Bio – A sideways spin performed while horizontal.

Mute – Grabbing the opposite skate with your arm going across the front of your body.

Late – Tricks performed closer to landing, which score more respect.

When you first enter a skate park it seems like complete chaos. There are people flipping tricks and pulling airs all over the place. But, there is order in the disorder and it pays to hang back for a while to see what is going on. Park Life Rules (right) will help you figure it out.

Mini ramp

A smaller version of the vert ramp, usually about 6 ft high and definitely the place to start.

Street course

Usually the largest area of the park. Around the edge are hips, quarter pipes and roll-ins. In the middle are fun boxes and rails.

Vert ramp

The big half pipe can be anything from 8–15 ft top to bottom; not for the faint hearted.

Competitions

Aggressive skate competitions are fun for bladers of all abilities. Competitors see them as a chance to find out how good they really are. For spectators, competitions are places to meet old friends and keep up with the latest tricks and fashions. For sponsors, they are the perfect places to get their products seen and identified with success.

A big crowd watches an outdoor competition in the sunshine.

What to expect at a competition:

1 Turn up and register. You will be given a number.

2 Your number will be called with about 20 other bladers for a 20-minute street-skating practice session.

3 When everyone has practised, qualifying runs will be held.

4 Those who qualify will then skate two runs of one minute each in the final.

5 After the street competition has finished there will probably be a mini-ramp comp and a vert comp.

6 All the scores are counted and a winner is announced for each section. The winners are showered with prizes and products from sponsors. Possibly.

Getting a sponsor

Doing well in competitions is the best way to attract a sponsor's attention, but not the only way. Getting on with other bladers and practising hard are other ways to attract the interest of sponsors. It's not just big manufacturers who sponsor bladers; your local skate shop might also be a source of sponsorship.

Indoor and undercover competitions can go ahead whatever the weather.

Top five heroes

- Arlo Eisenburg (U.S.A.).
- Jess Dyrenforth (G.B.).
- Chris Edwards (U.S.A.).
- Champion Baumstimler (U.S.A.).
- Rene Hulgreen (Denmark).

STREET SKATING

Street skating is the original form of aggressive blading. Indoor skate parks are good places to hold competitions and to use blades when the rain is pouring, but some bladers are never seen there. These are the hard-core street bladers.

Nicky Webster: Royale grind with the Houses of Parliament, London in the background.

As well as the skills needed to do 'sick' tricks, street bladers also have to deal with problems like bad weather, traffic and the general public. There are no judges to please; the pleasures of street skating are pure fun and the respect of other bladers.

5 all-time classic blading videos

- *The Hoax 2*
- *Dare to Air*
- *VG3*
- *Damaged Goods*
- *The Adventures of Mr Moosenuckle*

Rawlinson Rivera is picked out by the camera's flash.

Twilight lights up Simon Catford's grind for the audience.

Street survival kit

Things to have in your rucksack:

- Some antiseptic plasters.

- Shoes and, if possible, a mobile phone.

- Take plenty of fluid, especially if the sun is out or it's hot.

- A couple of spare bearings: if a bearing disintegrates while you are out, it can ruin a session.

- A blade tool. These combine allen keys, bearing pushers and any number of other useful tools.

- Take bus or cab fare. If you take a big slam, you might not feel like skating home.

23

Pioneers and heroes

Arlo Eisenburg.

Despite having been one of the pioneers of aggressive blading in the 1980s, Arlo still skates at a high level.

Arlo Eisenburg

One of the all-time great pioneers of aggressive skating is Arlo Eisenburg. Together he and Chris Edwards were among the very first people to skate in a style that had more to do with skateboarding than ice skating. Arlo adapted his skates so that he could perform grinds, and was one of the first bladers to be into jumps and airs.

Chris Edwards

Chris Edwards started blading when he was 13. At first he skated near his home in Escondido, U.S.A., but was soon signed-up to skate for team Rollerblade. 'I just wanted someone else to ride with,' he says. The first in-line competitions were anything but competitive – Chris won them all. He excels on the big half pipe; at his best, he amazed judges with his massive, contorted airs. Having once said, 'I will skate forever', he is still regularly placed in the top ten at competitions.

Angie Walton and Daily Bread Magazine

In 1994 Angie Walton started *Daily Bread Magazine*. The aim of the magazine was to give bladers the chance to control the direction of the growing sport, and take control away from skate manufacturers. In the past, some major skate manufacturers were even denied a mention in the magazine. *Daily Bread* is still flourishing as the leading aggressive skate magazine, with Angie Walton running it.

Chris Edwards high above the half pipe.

Blade Hockey

Blades were born out of the ice hockey scene, so it is no surprise that hockey is still part of the sport of blading. The rules of the game are based on ice hockey, with a few adjustments. Any blader with a basic knowledge of how to skate can play hockey. Two of the all-time greats of the NHL, Wayne Gretzky and Brett Hull, promote blading as an accompaniment to playing ice hockey.

A fully padded blade hockey player.

Club hockey rules:

- Mandatory protection: helmet, elbow pads, gloves, kneepads, shin guards and gum shield. Goalkeepers require extra protection.

- No charging, tripping or roughing.

- No holding on to feet, hands or sticks.

- No interfering with a player who doesn't have the puck.

Pucks.

Glove.

Stick.

Knee and
shin guard.

Standard helmet (Goalie's
helmet shown on page 10).

Chest and
shoulder padding.

Basic knockabout hockey requirements:

- Normal recreational skating kit (see page 10).
- One stick per player.
- A crushed drinks can, to use as a puck.

Ethics and Quiz

Blading is a fun sport, and it should be carried out with a smile. When blading around other people, remember that the reason that there are relatively few rules to follow is because everyone tries to get on with each other. Give everyone around you the respect that they deserve. As you become more experienced, remember how you felt when you were a beginner and try to give a bit of help to people who are just taking up the sport.

You are blading behind a crowd of pedestrians, do you?

A: Shout, so that they move out of your way.

B: Push them gently to one side.

C: Slow down and follow behind until you can pass safely.

While blading you find yourself at the top of a hill that is much steeper than you can deal with. Do you?

A: Keep going and sort out any problems later.

B: Stop and put on more protection.

C: Stop and remove your skates.

You see a beginner having problems, do you?

A: Stop and laugh.

B: Turn up your personal stereo.

C: Stop and give some advice.

How did you do?

Mostly A: You should consider taking up meditation rather than blading.

Mostly B: You have the right idea but you should work on your inter-personal skills.

Mostly C: You will be an asset to the blading scene – blade in peace.

Glossary

Word:	Means:	Doesn't Mean:
Air	A jump performed on blades.	Stuff you breathe.
Bearings	Tiny metal balls that allow wheels to spin more freely.	Positional guides.
Cruise	Gentle blading session, taking your time to get from one place to the next.	Holiday on board ship.
Deflectors	Things that protect the bolts on the chassis of your blades.	Obscure punk band.
Edged	Describes a turn that uses the edges of the wheels.	Moved cautiously along a narrow ledge.
Fakie	Describes any trick done while moving/rolling backwards.	Pretender.
Grind	A trick in which the chassis of the blade is used to slide along a wall's corner or a hand rail, for example.	Pulverise.
Half pipe	A large, steep, double-sided ramp on which bladers (and skateboarders and BMXers) perform tricks.	Broken drain.
Heel brake	A block of soft, rubbery plastic on the heel of a blade that allows bladers to slow down.	Fracture bone in heel.
Power slide	An advanced braking technique (see page 13 for a photo).	Loss of power.
T-stop	An advanced braking technique, where the blader drags his or her foot sideways to slow down.	Rest for cuppa.

Further Information

Books to read

In-Line Skating (Watts, 1998). *Superactiv: In-Line Skating* (Hodder Childrens Books, 1999). Most big bookshops have a selection of titles on blading, ranging from technique guides for beginners to technical manuals.

The Internet

Most of the big skate companies have their own websites: key the company name into a search engine to get there. These sites often have information on riders, new products and links to other blading sites.

You can also just key 'in-line skating' into a local search engine and get a list of on-line resources. These appear and disappear very quickly, which is why we haven't listed any specific sites here.

World records

World 1-hour record: In Feb 1991, Eddy Matzger (U.S.A.), at Long Beach, California, skated 34.82 km in 1 hour.

World 12-hour record: In Feb 1991, Jonathan Seutter (U.S.A.), at Long Beach, California, skated 285.86 km in 12 hours.

Index

Picture Acknowledgements
The publishers would like to thank the
following for giving their permission for
photos to be used in this book: all photos
supplied by Ben Roberts.